MEETING JEHOVAH'S WITNESSES

MEETING THE OTHERS

MEETING JEHOVAH'S WITNESSES *by Jack Roundhill*
MEETING SCHOOLS OF ORIENTAL MEDITATION *by Herbert Slade*
MEETING THE OCCULT *by Basil Wilby*
MEETING THE MORMONS by *Jack Roundhill*

MEETING JEHOVAH'S WITNESSES

by

JACK ROUNDHILL

LUTTERWORTH EDUCATIONAL

GUILDFORD & LONDON

First published 1973

This impression 1977

ISBN 0 7188 2009 6

Printed in Great Britain by The Bowering Press, Plymouth

CONTENTS

PREFACE

WHATEVER part of the world you live in, it is difficult *not* to meet Jehovah's Witnesses, because their emphasis is strong on witness as well as on Jehovah. They carry out their witness in market-places and from public platforms and wherever they can find an audience. But the characteristic method of the Witnesses is to take their message right into the house of anyone who will let them in. Often they get no further than the doorstep, and if so, they will use the doorstep as their pulpit. Often they are rebuffed, insulted, offered physical violence; but whatever their reception the JWs, with patience, resolution and sometimes rudeness go about their main business of door-to-door evangelism.

But what kind of evangelism? And what kind of evangelists? Are we to think of them as people who (because they are misguided) use dubious and sometimes offensive methods to preach the gospel of Jesus which all Christians, however ineffectively, try to commend? Christians are often perplexed by the Witnesses; are they allies to be befriended?—or enemies to be repulsed? Are they, indeed, fellow-Christians?

The JWs are not at all perplexed as to who their allies and their enemies are. They regard the rest of us (all of us) as either allies or dupes of the Arch-enemy of mankind, Satan, the Devil. They, they think, and they alone, are the Christians.

There are many reasons why JWs arouse curiosity, even wonder, and possibly admiration. Here are some of them:

1 They are definitely different. They don't have the same message or the same methods as other religious bodies known to us. They don't even have the same 'style of life'—no Christmas, not even birthday parties.

Although they brandish the Bible they seem as alien as Muslims or Buddhists in their way of thinking.

2 They are so assiduous in their doorstep evangelism. In this country with a population of around fifty million there are less than 70,000 JWs. And yet most of us have had them on our doorstep, perhaps many times. This indicates an efficient organisation as well as burning enthusiasm.

3 They show a detailed knowledge of the Bible. They can quote it and find their way easily about it. Their ordinary members seem to be extraordinarily well trained.

4 They interest a section of the population which is badly represented in the Christian denominations. No one can sneer at the JWs as being a 'middle-class' movement.

5 It really is a 'movement'. In one hundred years of existence there is hardly a country in the world that it has not penetrated. It has branches everywhere, from the tiny sheikhdom of Abu Dhabi where there are three members in a population of twelve thousand, to the Republic of Zambia where one in eighty-eight is a JW. It publishes its literature in no less than 150 different languages and dialects.

So much of the teaching of Jehovah's Witnesses is to me not only false but abhorrent and loathsome (they start with a God who has it in mind to destroy the rest of us in a particularly horrible way), but I can't deny that I have grown to like many of them as individuals and may even say that I have made a few friends.

In the years that I have been interested in them and their New World Society I have never failed to receive a welcome at their meetings, assemblies and sacraments, and I have always found someone willing and ready to answer my (sometimes impertinent) questions. This is in spite of an unrelenting hostility to the Christian Church and clergy which is shown in their lectures and publications. I am grateful for their kindness to this clergyman and if I have misrepresented or misunderstood them in any way I shall be glad if they will tell me where they think I have gone wrong. If I have been unkind or unfair I hope they will forgive me.

Because their teaching seems to be, in my judgement, such a distorted travesty of the Christian Faith, I must declare emphatically where I stand; but I have an ungrudging respect for many of those who hold it and this respect is bound to show through. To some readers my effort may seem inadequate as an attack on the Witnesses, and so it is. My first aim is to understand rather than to oppose or discredit.

Nevertheless, in trying to share an understanding of the JWs I hope I may succeed in dissuading any who might be toying with the idea of joining them.

JACK ROUNDHILL

Dorking, 1973

1

WHAT THEY BELIEVE

Christians should not necessarily believe all that the enemies of the Jehovah's Witnesses say of them.

JEHOVAH'S WITNESSES have many diverse abilities but they seem to have a positive gift for bringing out the worst in people. This happens when people who, in normal circumstances, are well-mannered and polite, find at their door two JWs, eager to speak and commend their faith. Mild Christian people have been known to slam the door in the faces of these unwelcome callers.

Nor have Christian writers always found it possible to be charitable to these people. Horton Davies, in his *Christian Deviations*, says of C. T. Russell, 'Russell is a curiously disreputable figure to have originated a new religious Movement. So overweening was his egotism that he claimed to be a competent Greek scholar, though, as was proved in court, he did not know a letter of the alphabet of that language. His domineering conceit and wayward affections became widely known when his wife sued him for divorce and her petition was readily granted. . . . He was also believed to have played upon the fears of sick persons to induce them to make over their fortunes to his organisation. . . .' Kenneth Ross in one of his pamphlets declares that Russell 'was a fraudulent businessman, and was divorced by his wife for adultery'.

A Presbyterian publication quotes an Australian journalist's view of Rutherford as 'Bishop of bunk, religious racketeer, proprietor of the biggest door-to-door book-pushing ramp in the world, virtuoso of radio and gramophone mental vapour and apostle of sectarian prurience', and it goes on to say of the publications of the Society that they 'pervert the Scriptures and make downright denial of Christian truth, they exhibit malice and censoriousness and come near to sedition-mongering, they inculcate exclusiveness, pride and religious snobbery.'

The most frequent accusation levelled against the Society is that it is 'in it for the money' and that the sale of publications is building up a huge fortune for someone, somewhere. There was a time when it was believed that the best way to commend Christianity was to decry the motives of other religions. Nowadays we treat Buddhism and Islam with proper respect but often fail to attempt the same for the New World Society.

Honesty alone demands that we should not believe the extreme accusations. Starting with Russell—it is quite true that his wife divorced him but there is no valid evidence that he ever committed adultery; he did not claim (as far as we can discover) to know either Greek or Hebrew but to know enough of the alphabets of these languages to be able to refer to a Greek or Hebrew lexicon. No one has proved that he took large sums of money for his personal use, and JW sources claim that, with his wife's consent, he gave to the organisation the proceeds of the sale of his father's drapery stores, a total of 250,000 dollars, a considerable sum in those days. We know much less about Judge Rutherford. All that can be claimed is that he was an able, ruthless administrator, and that he lived in some comfort in the Society's west coast mansion.

How are the early leaders regarded by the JWs today? I asked one of the officers at their London headquarters what they thought of Mr Russell and if they had any comments about the stories of commercial dishonesty and marital infidelity which have been told about him. The officer told me, 'The answer can be summarised in this way: (a) We want to be judged on our message alone—is it true or is it not? And we want to be judged not on account of one man and his doings but on account of what the Bible says. (b) A great many untruths have been put forward about Pastor Russell both in his public and private life, but I will tell you this—when his wife was in court she was directly asked by counsel, "Do you accuse your husband of having committed adultery?" and she said, "No, I do not." That is on the court record and we are glad to quote it. (c) We believe that we have learned a good deal since Pastor Russell's day; Jehovah God is still revealing things to us and we do not base our doctrines on the teaching of one man alone.' As regards Rutherford, in his book, *Jehovah's Witnesses*, Marley Cole (a member of the Society) does not try to hide the ruthless way in which Rutherford took over the leadership. It is fair to say that although the two pioneers are revered, they are not regarded in any way as infallible, either in their lives or in their teaching.

There is no substance in the allegation that members of the Society are actuated by personal financial gain. The gain that they seek is in the coming Kingdom and in hope of this they forgo earthly aggrandisement. Some of their workers give time to the organisation at a rate of pay which even the Salvation Army would not consider excessive. The 'pioneers' undertake to spend one hundred hours a month on 'publishing' plus time for meetings and for study—this does not allow them much time to earn more than a bare living. The 'special pioneers' who work full-time for the Society are paid (in 1972) seventeen pounds a month, and they usually find it necessary to attach themselves to some faithful family in order to survive at all.

Far from condemning them for their avarice, we can admire the JWs for their indifference to money and acknowledge that they may well set an example to the rest of us.

As far as the Society itself is concerned in this matter, we can be similarly admiring. Far back in 1879 the *Watchtower* advertised a new hymn book, asking readers to send for it. They were told: 'If you can afford and desire to pay for it you may do so'. This is not the attitude of an organisation interested primarily in money.

Another *Watchtower* in the same year asked for subscriptions but said: 'Do not suppose these remarks to be an appeal for money. No. *Zion's Watch Tower* (this was the original name of the magazine) has, we believe, Jehovah for its backer, and while this is the case it will never beg nor petition men for support. When He who says "All the gold and the silver of the mountains are mine" fails to provide necessary funds we will understand it to be time to suspend the publication.'

We cannot but applaud the record of unflinching bravery shown by JWs in Hitler's concentration camps. No-one has ever disputed this. It is even said that their courage and witness were such that there were cases of SS guards who were so moved as to join the ranks of the JWs and to take their place among the prisoners. Sometimes their courage was called out by some matter which would, for others, hardly count as principle at all. We know that the Witnesses believe it to be God's Will that they should neither accept blood-transfusion or consume blood in any form; we are told that in conditions of appalling hardship prisoners were offered twice a week, as part of their meagre diet, a slice of blood-sausage, but this the JWs refused, and inevitably brought themselves one step nearer death by starvation.

I would agree with David and Margaret Phypers (*The Christian Graduate*, December, 1970) who say that the 'Witnesses are not evil or deliberately sinister in their work and methods. They are exceptionally upright people, very sincere, yet sadly misguided.'

Jehovah's Witnesses are like people who are waiting for a bomb to explode. They are living under pressure and are impelled by a desperate sense of urgency. They believe it is their duty to warn as many people as possible of the disaster—and the opportunity—which is about to befall the human race. They are eager to save thousands—millions—for the millenium, before it is too late. There are three parts to their message:

1 *The world as we know it is doomed* The world we live in is dominated by Satan. He is the 'god of this world' and all governments and political structures of every kind are subject to his evil power. But (say the JWs) Satan's time is running out, Jehovah God is preparing to defeat him and his minions at a horrific show-down, a battle of cosmic proportions, called Armageddon. This battle will be followed by a renewed earth, bountiful and freed from Satan's power, which will last for a thousand splendid years. This they call the Kingdom, the Millenium or the New World.

2 *Only Jehovah's Witnesses have the key to salvation* The established Christian churches can't save anyone. They are powerless to help. In fact the denominations are themselves part of Satan's empire and, like the rest of it, are doomed to destruction. People who look to the church to save them are leaning on a broken reed; the church has no part in the Kingdom. There is no political solution which can aid mankind, and the United Nations is singled out for special attack.

3 *Join the Society before it is too late* Everyone who wants to share in the Kingdom must join the New World Society. His duty as a JW must be to study the Bible in conjunction with the Society's publications and

strive with all his energy to pass the message on to others. Everything else in his life must be subordinate to this, family, friends, daily work and current interests.

As they peddle this uncompromising message it is not surprising that JWs find themselves unpopular. They can hardly be admired and applauded by those who live comfortably in the world which they so roundly condemn. When we have commended their persistence, their enthusiasm, their dogged energy in doorstep visiting, we have perhaps commended all that there is to be commended.

Or have they a secret which Christians would do well to learn? To answer this question it is necessary to look at some of the tenets of this faith in more detail.

Armageddon

Since JWs began, a hundred years ago, they have steadfastly maintained that humanity is on the very brink of Armageddon—the end of the world. In the first number of the *Watchtower* magazine (July 1879) readers were told: 'We are living "in the last days"—"the day of the Lord"—"the end" of the Gospel age, and consequently, in the dawn of the new age.'

In the nineteen-twenties their message was the same. 'Millions now living', trumpeted their slogan, 'will never die!'

Generation after generation of JWs has arisen and has preached the imminence of the end of all things. Undaunted by the experience of the past, JWs of the nineteen-seventies still maintain that 'there is not long to go'. It is widely believed in the Society that Armageddon will overtake the world before this decade ends.

Why are the JWs so sure? They tell us that Jesus has given us, in Matthew 24: 7, a clear description of the year 1914: 'Nation will rise against nation, and kingdom against kingdom, and there will be famines and earthquakes in various places.' They catalogue all the wars and natural disasters which have occurred on earth since that date and ask: 'Is it not obvious that the time of the end is almost upon us?'

They may also quote some words of Jesus from the same chapter of Matthew: 'This generation will not pass away until all these things have taken place', and the JW will tell you that Jesus was referring, not to the generation of those who stood around him at the time, but to the generation of people who were alive in 1914.

Since the days of Pastor Russell who thought that the world would end in 1914, this date has had a fascination for JWs. The fact that it saw the outbreak of World War I has been sufficient to convince them that it is the key-point in determining the date of Armageddon.

Armageddon is the name which JWs give to a terrible battle which will be fought on this earth between Jehovah God and the forces of Satan. This battle will not be fought by earthly armies (it is not, for example, a Third World War) but is to be a conflict between good and evil on the spiritual plane. God's armies, under the command of Jesus, will win a resounding victory over evil. In spite of its spiritual character, Armageddon will bring physical death and destruction in its wake. All who do not belong to the New World Society will be attacked by a macabre flesh-eating plague which will consume them as they stand on their feet. After the battle, the fortunate survivors will go out and see layers of dead bodies, swarming with worms, piled high on the surface of the earth.

Shortly afterwards (say the Witnesses) birds and animals will come and eat up the rotting flesh, leaving the bones to be buried by members of the Society. This will take no less than seven months to complete, and the next task, the tearing down of the ruins of the old world, will take seven years.

All is now set for the New World that is dawning; and what a world that is going to be!

Before we describe it we should outline what is going on in the spiritual and heavenly realms. The first and most important consequence of Armageddon is that the Devil, who has been teasing and tormenting the world, causing sorrow and sin and every imaginable evil, will be chained up, rendered powerless and hurled into the abyss for a thousand years. He will have no power to hurt or harm the New World until the thousand years have come to an end.

A certain number of selected individuals, 144,000 of them, will be taken by Jesus Christ to govern with him in heaven, and they are known to the Society as the 'little flock'. We know nothing (say the JWs) of their life-style or what heaven will be like. All we know is that of all men and women they are most to be envied.

The others who survive the catastrophe, however, have no need to be downhearted. For them, earth itself will be transformed into a kind of heaven with every pleasure and privilege that the heart could desire.

All those who inherit this idyllic New World will set their hands to building a paradise on earth. There will be no crime, no hunger, no evil thoughts, no bad breath. Wild beasts will wander around at will but they will cause harm to no-one, and the lion and the lamb will lie down together. Wrinkles of care and age will be smoothed away, grey hair will have its youthful colour restored and a surge of perfect health will invigorate the flesh with supernal youth.

Many faithful people from the past will be raised from the dead to join the paradisal community, and babies will continue to be born until the population reaches a comfortable level for the resources of the renewed earth. When this point has been reached, human reproduction will cease.

Other factors will allay fears of the consequences of over-population. Enough food will be supplied because every plant will be more fruitful than human beings can at present imagine, and the land will overflow with rich abundance. It is declared, without emotion, that the land will have been enriched by the corpses of those who fell at Armageddon. There will be no weeds, plant diseases or destructive pests. If necessary, new continents will rise from the sea-bed to provide new and fertile land to accommodate the population.

As if this is not sufficient for the most capacious cup of happiness, we are given one more assurance: there will be no trades unions in the New World, nor will there be any employers' organisations, for every man will work for himself and for his family.

There is one dark cloud on the horizon of this sunny world and it cannot fail to get larger as the time goes by. It is the knowledge that the idyllic state can last no longer than a thousand years. The Devil and his demons will be chained up after Armageddon for a long, but limited time, and when it comes to an end, the Devil will be set free to vex the inhabitants with sore trials and temptations, which will bring death to very many.

The Bible

Nobody can deny that the JWs use the Bible a great deal. It provides them with a useful opening topic when they begin a doorstep conversation in a Christian country. Their speakers quote it in their public addresses and their literature is liberally bespattered with references to biblical texts.

They give the impression that they take the Bible very seriously, and it is undoubtedly true that their members have a better working knowledge of the texts of scripture than can be claimed by the members of any major Christian denomination. As the Witnesses expound the distinctive doctrines of their sect, they skilfully slot in Bible texts, which give an apparent authority to their claims.

It is not surprising then, that many simple people have been misled into thinking that, because the JWs use their Bibles so frequently and with such flourish, they speak with the authentic voice of scripture itself. Let us, therefore, have a look at the use which Witnesses make of the Bible.

They use their own literature (*Watchtower*, *Awake!*, pamphlets and hard-back publications) as primary, and pick out selected Bible texts to back up their teaching. It may just be said that this is a temptation to which many earnest Christians have succumbed—that of searching for 'proof-texts'—but in the case of the Witnesses it has been carried to extreme lengths. They are reluctant to use the Bible without a great deal of written or spoken commentary, and they have erected many an involved and complicated doctrine on the basis of an isolated text. The whole concept of Armageddon, for example, is based on Revelation 16: 14, 16.

They pay special attention to those books of the Bible which have, it must be acknowledged, been the playground of cranks and fanatics for many a long day. There are undoubted difficulties in understanding much of such books as Daniel and Ezekiel in the Old Testament, and Revelation in the New Testament; these writings contain a great deal of fantastic imagery and symbolism which it is not easy to fathom. There have always been men who have claimed to be able to interpret them, and from these books have come many fanciful distortions which have intrigued and sometimes captivated men's minds.

In a later chapter we shall see some specific examples of the curious and arbitrary way in which the Witnesses interpret scripture. For the present, let us acknowledge that the Bible is a large book with such an abundant wealth of symbolism (some of which, however clear it might be to the writer and the first readers, is admittedly mystifying to us), that it is possible to see what one wants to see and to prove what one wants to prove from it. This is especially so if texts are taken out of their historical context and divorced from the situation for which they were originally written.

The basic claim of the Witnesses is that the true meaning of scripture has been completely hidden from mankind for nearly two thousand years. After the death of the apostles (they say) the Bible was treasured and read, but until Jehovah God began to reveal its inner meaning to Pastor Russell in the nineteenth century, it was as obscure as is a book in an unknown tongue.

Since Mr Russell's day, JWs believe that God has been disclosing more and more of the Bible's true meaning. Mr Russell himself quoted the Bible a great deal, but it is also true that he attempted to establish certain of his key doctrines from the internal measurements of the Great Pyramid. His successor, Judge Rutherford, repudiated this with a warning that all doctrines must be derived from the Bible and the Bible alone. We are bound to say that Mr Rutherford was not consistently loyal to his own principles. For example, he maintains the position (derived from neither the Bible nor the Great Pyramid!) that the Star of Bethlehem mentioned in Matthew's Gospel was motivated by demonic forces and that the Wise Men were, wittingly or unwittingly, tools of the Devil!

It is difficult to argue with those who rely on unsupported assertions and it is not surprising that Christians find it difficult to discuss the Bible in an intelligent way with JWs. Discussions make no progress unless the Society's assumptions and assertions are unquestioned. It may encourage those who take issue with them to remember that no Christian denomination, and no independent biblical scholar, agrees with the distinctive interpretations of the JWs, or indeed, commends the translation of scripture which they use.

Jesus

It is traditional Christian belief that Jesus is on the same plane of being as God the Father; that Jesus was 'with God' (John 1: 1) in the very beginning, and that from the beginning the Word (i.e. Jesus) 'was God'. Christians have a similar belief about the Holy Spirit and they express their teaching about God in a summary known as the doctrine of the Trinity.

Christians also believe that Jesus lived on earth as a man—a genuine human being—and that his birth, life, death and resurrection took place as an essential part of God's plan for the redemption of humanity.

JWs reject the doctrine of the Trinity and they think of Jesus, not as God nor, indeed, as man, but as a super-angelic being. Far from being the 'only-begotten' Son of God, they affirm that at the beginning of Creation God created *two* sons, the first of whom was Jesus, the Word, whom they identify with Michael, the Archangel, the leader of the angels (the good 'spirit-creatures').

The second son was Lucifer, who was later to rebel against God, and would, under the name of Satan the Devil, rule over the kingdoms of this world as Commander of the forces of evil, the demons, or bad 'spirit-creatures'.

Having identified Jesus with Michael, the JWs turn to Daniel 9: 24–27 and assert that they can deduce from this the year of Jesus' birth at Bethlehem, which they set at 2 B.C. on or about 1st October. In the year A.D. 29 and at the age of thirty (they tell us), at his baptism Jesus was appointed king and messiah. The events of our Lord's ministry (as seen by JWs) call for no further comment except that in recent years they have pronounced that Jesus died, not on a cross but on a 'torture-stake' with no cross-piece. The most significant action of Jesus on earth, say the Witnesses was that he went about making known the name of God, that is, declaring God's name as Jehovah (or, perhaps, Yahweh). This they derive from a literal interpretation of John 17: 26.

They say (as Christians do) that after the crucifixion Jesus rose from the dead and returned to heaven. Then, in the year 1914, he was invested with kingly power and began to take charge of his kingdom. This action of Jesus (or Michael) aroused the envy and wrath of Lucifer(or Satan, the Devil) who then attempted to 'eat up' the kingdom while it was still in its infancy. The Devil perceived that the power which he had held for so long was now threatened and his strenuous efforts to devour the new kingdom are described (so the Witnesses believe) in Revelation 12: 7–9, in symbolic imagery. The Devil's efforts, however, were in vain. Although he will not be subdued until the coming Armageddon, for him 1914 was the beginning of the end. Four years later, to confirm that he was now taking charge, Jesus cleansed the heavenly temple of God.

The assertions of the Witnesses about the supposed activity of Jesus and the Devil in the spiritual and heavenly realms, rest upon no firmer foundation than wild imaginings. The year 1914 has a special significance for the Society, and it dates back to the days of their founder, but it has no more connection with the Bible in general or the Book of Revelation in particular than any other year, and no acknowledged Bible scholar can be found to support their interpretations.

The JWs claim that the present time is crucial. Humanity is on the brink of impending Armageddon when Jesus will vanquish the Devil and his demon hordes, chaining him up and hurling him down to the abyss. But in the meantime Satan is still at large, troubling and tempting mankind, wielding fearfully the last remnants of his declining power.

Their Founders

The story of the JWs begins with a man named Charles Taze Russell, who was born in Pittsburgh in 1852. From an early age he had a lively interest in religious questions. As a young man, Russell refused to accept the doctrine of eternal punishment as it was expounded by the preachers of his day, and he left the Presbyterian church in which he had been brought up, and joined the Congregationalists for a time. He also attached himself to the Adventists and he absorbed some of their teaching about the Second Coming of Our Lord. In 1872 he published a pamphlet which claimed that our Lord's return could be expected in 1874 and that the end of the world would take place in 1914. Russell was a powerful orator and his magnetic personality began to attract a large number of followers; when the year 1874 brought no open and visible return of Christ, he was able to satisfy them by claiming that it had been a secret and invisible event.

He was tireless in his efforts to gain adherents and in 1879 he founded a periodical, *Zion's Watch Tower*, a magazine which he edited for thirty-seven years and which survives and flourishes to this day.

Russell, like many of those who were to follow him, seems to have been a somewhat credulous person, and his energy and enthusiasm in early years were not always wisely directed. His enemies have seized on several ventures which seem to reflect on his integrity; at various times he promoted Miracle Wheat ('will yield up to 250 bushels an acre'), Wonderful Cottonseed ('will revolutionise the cotton industry'), Millennial beans ('set five of these and provide your family with food for a year'), and Santonine ('simple cure for appendicitis symptoms . . . also for typhoid fever which is also a worm disease') as well as a cure for cancer.

By his tireless activity, his voluminous writings and his lecture tours, Russell built up an organisation which quickly spread across the world, and its international headquarters was set up in Brooklyn in 1909. His death in 1916 was a blow to the Society and there was some unhappy confusion until after some intrigue and controversy, 'Judge' Rutherford took over the reins of power. His previous position had been that of legal adviser to the Society.

Rutherford had his own doctrinal emphases and he dealt sharply with those who resented the new theological approach. It was under his direction that the name 'Jehovah's Witnesses' was adopted (formerly 'Bible Students' or more popularly 'Russellites') and he worked resolutely to extend the Society's empire still further. In the early days of his leadership, he was committed with six subordinates to a twenty-year prison sentence, and it seemed as if the Movement might collapse. The charge was 'conspiring to cause insubordination in the military forces' and was due to their encouragement of members to take a practical pacifist position. In the event, the leader and his colleagues made a successful appeal and emerged from gaol after a period of nine months. The general impression is that the sentence was not long enough to cause any damage, but long enough to provide useful publicity and an aura of martyrdom, which gave the movement a much-needed shot in the arm. Since those days it has never looked back.

Like his predecessor, Rutherford poured out volume after volume. In 1940 he claimed to have written ninety-nine books and pamphlets in the previous twenty years, and he continued to add to the number up to the time of his death in 1942. His writings, it is said, have appeared in seventy-eight languages and over 300 million items have been distributed.

Since Rutherford, the President of the Watch Tower Society has been

Nathan Homer Knorr, who was born on St George's Day, 1905. The Presidency is a lifetime appointment.

Organisation

Jehovah's Witnesses in Britain are controlled from the London headquarters at Mill Hill, although all major policy is determined by the governing body, which meets periodically in Brooklyn, New York. For ease of administration, Britain is divided into districts, each of which is in the care of a district overseer. Each district is further divided into about twelve circuits, making a total of about sixty circuits in this country. Immediately below the circuit is the local congregation, of which there are about nine hundred.

To complete the statistics, one could add that Jehovah's Witnesses in the United Kingdom number about 64,000 members, and they claim that the total is rising at a rate of about five per cent each year. The number of those baptised in 1971 is given as 5,177. The world-wide attendance at the 'Memorial' (the annual commemoration of the Last Supper) in 1972 was 3,662,407.

The effective unit of the Society is the congregation, and it is organised as a preaching and evangelistic force in the community. It exists to instruct all its members in the content of the Society's faith, and to equip them for their task of passing it on to others. Every member is regarded as sharing to the full in this evangelistic responsibility, and to this end, they avoid using the word 'member', and refer to 'publishers' or (within the Movement) 'brothers and sisters'. They can even tell us (they claim) the total number of hours spent on their primary, evangelistic, door-to-door work in any given year, and the number of hours spent on 'back-calls' (i.e. follow-ups). In 1971 these were 11,859,342 and 6,145,189 respectively.

The Society repudiates any distinction between ministers and lay members, and it is partly on the grounds that every Witness is a minister (not on grounds of pacifism) that they refuse to serve in the armed forces. However, there are some signs that a ministerial class is emerging at the present time.

Within the congregation they have begun to distinguish 'elders', a group of mature, responsible men, from whom the main office-bearers are drawn (i.e. the 'congregation servant', the 'assistant congregation servant', the 'Bible study servant') and if there are sufficient elders, the 'Watchtower study servant' and the 'theocratic ministry school servant', the latter being a training officer. The chairman of the body of elders is the congregation servant, and this office is held for one year at a time, beginning on October 1. The other group within the membership is that of 'ministerial servants' who arrange for literature supplies, assign 'preaching territory', and look after the accounts. They also look after the Kingdom Hall (its cleaning and maintenance), keep records of attendance and make sure that newcomers are welcomed, and records kept up to date.

Certain dedicated Witnesses, known as 'Pioneers', undertake to spend one hundred hours a month in publishing duties, in addition to their attendances at meetings. They receive no payment and they support themselves as best they can. There are also 'special pioneers' who devote all their time to the Society, and they may be sent anywhere and asked to do anything. Special pioneers spend one hundred and fifty hours a month in publishing.

Rallies are held twice yearly so that a circuit may draw together its total membership, and district assemblies are held from time to time. Every so often, large and impressive national and international conventions are held, and members are expected to obtain leave from their daily occupations to attend. As far back as 1910 the JWs had 8,000 inside the Albert Hall for such an assembly, and another 5,000 were accommodated at an overflow meeting.

The Witnesses make a special point of perfection in organising these conventions, and give a minute attention to detail, so much so, that representatives of the British Army are said to have attended some of them to make a study of the planning, and in particular, the provision of cooked meals for such large numbers.

A notable convention was held at the Rugby Football Ground at Twickenham in 1963, when meetings were attended by up to 50,000 people. An earlier conference held at Nuremburg had an attendance of twice this number, 40,000 of whom were resident in a town of tents, with piped water, sanitary arrangements, a post office and elaborate arrangements for convenience and comfort.

As numbers grow, international assemblies present considerable difficulties, and at the time of writing nothing is known of future plans; the last one was held at Wembley in 1969, and the attendance was said to be 82,000.

Evangelism

A JW is usually recruited as a result of doorstep evangelism. Most worshippers in the churches have been 'brought up' in the faith which they now profess, but the typical JW is a convert from at least a nominal connection with some Christian denomination.

When a JW finds interest and questionings on one of his calls, he goes back and makes (as they say) a 'back-call'. He invites the enquirer to study the Bible with the help of Society literature, and after a few weeks may ask him to attend the local Kingdom Hall.

Here the newcomer receives a warm and friendly welcome and is initiated into the series of meetings and visits which make up the life of a JW.

The typical meeting time is on Sunday afternoons when the 'public meeting' takes place. It consists mainly of an address which is constructed from an outline sent down from headquarters and is delivered by one of the members, usually the congregation servant. After this there is a five-minute period for relaxation and general conversation, followed by the Bible study meeting. The Bible study meeting is actually a close study of the main article in the current number of *Watchtower*, with frequent reference to Bible texts. It is conducted by a question-and-answer technique and it evokes a great deal of audience participation. Hands are raised and those who give 'correct' answers ('correct' that is, according to *Watchtower* magazine) are commended; those who answer incorrectly are tactfully and politely handled.

Other meetings are the house Bible studies and the theocratic ministry school. The latter is described by Ruth Brandon as 'One of the most striking aspects of the whole Witness organisation. . . . perfectly normal, tongue-tied people, often uneducated and inarticulate, are taught to project themselves both on the doorstep and also in speaking *ex tempore* at meetings. . . . All Witnesses, as soon as they are old enough to read and speak, take part. The textbook of the school is a Witness publication called

Qualified to be Ministers and it is one of the best practical guides to public speaking I have seen.'

After a year or so as an active publisher it is suggested to the individual that he be baptised. Although baptism can take place in private (an invalid member can be baptised in a bath) it must be total immersion and it is usually carried out at one of the circuit or district assemblies, perhaps in a swimming-pool hired for the occasion.

As time goes on and progress is made in the theocratic ministry school, the JW may be invited to give the address at a public meeting, and if he is specially gifted and circumstances allow, he may take on the exacting and dedicated work of a pioneer. Or he may be asked to take on one of the posts of responsibility in the congregation.

Every JW, unless prevented by illness, will take part in the regular assemblies on circuit, district, national and international level. He is expected to get time off from work to attend the national assemblies, which may last several days and which are a source of great encouragement and enthusiasm for the Witness.

2

WHAT WE HAVE TO SAY

They are Separatists

IF Christmas Day falls on, say, a Tuesday, the JW will keep to his normal Tuesday routine. There will be nothing special on the dinner-table, no turkey or plum-pudding, but rissoles and chips or perhaps a pork chop. He may use part of the day for his publishing activities, and there might well be a Bible-study in the local Kingdom Hall. The Society goes to great lengths to discourage its adherents from keeping Christmas a festival, for which Judge Rutherford seems to have had a special dislike. We remember what he said about the Wise Men and the Star of Bethlehem.

There are many other ways in which JWs are encouraged to stand apart from the rest of mankind. They have even developed their own style of language, which separates them from other people, and an outsider will need to associate with JWs for some time if he wants to understand it. They speak of publishers rather than members, and they have Kingdom Halls rather than churches or chapels. They do not use such familiar terms as Old Testament and New Testament and, most striking of all, they speak of God as Jehovah God.

Their style of life is such as to make them as 'different' as possible, and it is not surprising that they do not celebrate birthdays. ('The only people in the Bible who kept birthdays were Pharaoh and Herod Antipas, both of whom followed false religion.')

There is, however, one major issue which, above all others, brings the Society into the public eye from time to time, and yet marks its members off from other people, Christian and non-Christian alike. It is the stand which they make against blood-transfusion. JWs are taught that if life is at stake, even when it is the life of one's wife or child, it is utterly and completely wrong to permit blood-transfusion. On this issue, as on many others, JWs stand firm and they succeed in wringing a reluctant admiration from those who disagree with them. It is unusual to discover that there are still people in the world who are prepared to die (or to allow members of their families to die) for what, to other people, is not a matter of principle at all.

It is difficult to know the real reason for the prohibition, but it is ostensibly based on the Old Testament regulation forbidding Israelites to consume blood, and which is expressed in Leviticus 17: 10.

In their attitude towards the State, JWs are different from other people. They do not vote nor are any JWs ambitious to become Members of Parliament. They forbid their members to take up arms in time of war, and they incurred a great deal of public odium during World War II by claiming their rights as conscientious objectors. It is interesting that their justification for this is mainly because to enrol in the armed forces would make one an active agent of the State which, according to their view, is part of the Devil's organisation. Under normal circumstances they are law-abiding people, and their conscience allows them to pay taxes and give reasonable obedience, on the grounds that even if God does not approve of the State, at least He permits it to exist.

As a consequence of their doctrine that Armageddon is just around the corner, they lay no stress on the importance of education, for themselves or for their children. Why should they? Their basic premiss is that the world as we know it will come to an end in the course of the next year or two—or even the next month or so. Why then should anyone embark on a course of training which he will not be able to use in the New World? It is important that children should learn to read and write, they can then read the Bible and begin to express themselves as faithful publishers, but too much training might only be a waste of time.

As a result of this same doctrine, some young married JWs have said that they do not intend to have children 'until after Armageddon'. After all, they do not think that there will be long to wait.

We do not, then, need to feel embarrassed or uncharitable if we find ourselves thinking that JWs are different from the majority of Christians, as different as another religion, like Islam, perhaps. They think of themselves as being different and separate, and they strive to be so. They *are* different, they have a different gospel, different methods, and a different pattern of life.

There is no false modesty about the Witnesses. They believe that they are different from everyone else because they alone are right. They (so they believe) are the chosen people of God and the only ones who can escape from the wrath to come. Believing this, it is surely to their credit that they strain every nerve to persuade the rest of us to join their Society. In a strange way, it is a mark of their kindly feeling towards us.

They are Authoritarian

Jehovah's Witnesses proclaim the sovereignty of God. The fact that they refer to him as *Jehovah* God gives us an indication that an Old Testament view of him is paramount. This God of theirs is distant, austere, and anyone who attends the assemblies of the Witnesses cannot fail to notice that there is very little sense of fellowship or communion with God, and He does not seem to be known to the Witnesses as a living Presence. They spend very little time in actual prayer to God and do not in practice encourage an intimate relationship, either on a congregational or a personal basis. God may be acknowledged as Creator and as law-giver, but an onlooker is bound to suspect that the whole of their attention is concentrated not on God at all, but on the New World Society to which they belong, and on the future which they believe lies in store for them. The Society itself is their god and, although they would hotly dispute this, it is to the Society that their lives are dedicated.

This is, perhaps, the key to their success. Many people today have lost all sense of 'belonging' to the neighbourhood in which they live; they feel that they have no real roots in any community and they feel a keen sense of loss. When they are asked to join the Witnesses they are made to feel wanted and they are given a sense of belonging, a set of rules to live by, and an over-riding sense of purpose in their lives. Every member is given a job to do and is made to feel a worthwhile member of a mighty team.

The JW is rewarded with a kind of security, but at tremendous cost. He finds himself part of an autocratic, authoritarian organisation which tells him in the most minute detail what he is to believe and in what way he is to serve God. The New World Society gives no opportunity to discuss or to argue, still less to disagree, and one who joins must accept, as if from God, the dogma and the discipline.

The dogma and the discipline are made known through the Society's publications and especially through *Watchtower* and its companion *Awake!* It is true that JWs know their Bibles, but they do so only as it is related to the New World doctrines; they are not encouraged to use standard independent Bible commentaries. 'Whatever they are,' says Ruth Brandon, 'they are not Bible students. They are *Watchtower* students. The Bible is used merely to illustrate and prove points made in the *Watchtower*.'

Who writes the *Watchtower* articles? According to a recent Yearbook we learn that they may be written anywhere in the world, but they are combed through at the Brooklyn headquarters for possible deviant thinking, and they are ultimately issued on the authority of the Society as a whole.

At the Watch Tower House in north-west London, they have a printing works which turns out English and European and some Asian editions, with smooth and seemingly effortless efficiency. English copies (as well as foreign ones for immigrant communities) are despatched in large green vans, which take them to every corner of the land. It is essential to the Society and a point of honour with its members that whatever strikes may be on in the world outside, nothing must stop the *Watchtower* from arriving on time. This is, for them, not just the Society's magazine, it is their regular message from God. One might almost say that it is this for which the whole organisation exists.

Most JWs are content to have it so; this is their idea of authentic religion. In his book *The Jehovah's Witnesses*, H. H. Stroup wrote: 'The fact that Witnesses are not called to participate in a genuinely democratic organisation seems in general to please them. The primary task of the individual believer is to trust and to trust again. He does not have to think about the running of the Movement. He does not have to share in formulating its policies or in creating new modes of action. All things come from the Society, and to the Society each individual believer owes his soul.'

The Society may have changed in some ways since Mr Stroup wrote in the 1940s, but it has not changed in this respect. As we turn the pages of

Watchtower, we see that some people are singled out and described as 'sheep-like'. We are filled with amazement when we realise that, in the eyes of the Society, this is not a condemnation but a compliment.

They Work on False Premisses

In September 1971, in the House of Commons, one MP (Mr Michael Stewart) said of another (Mr Enoch Powell):

> I always feel when listening to the Rt. Hon. Gentleman that it is like listening to an account of the effects of the working of the whole universe if we first grant the premiss that the moon is made of green cheese or that a circle has four corners. Granted these extraordinary premisses, it all follows with the most dazzling logic.

The JWs have a body of belief which is frighteningly complex and involved, yet with a certain internal logic about it; but it is based upon narrow assumptions. If you fail to grant the assumptions, the whole structure falls to the ground.

The first assumption (taken for granted by the Society) is that for 2,000 years, from the death of the last apostle to the utterances of Russell, God left himself without any effective witness in the world. They mention those 2,000 years of Christian history and civilisation, but regard them as a period when God had nothing to say, or perhaps, had no-one through whom he could say it. They believe that certain men had gleams of insight—Arius, Peter Waldo, Wycliffe and Luther—but these men were, in the last resort, lightweights. The revelation which closed at the end of New Testament times opened again when Charles Taze Russell spoke and wrote.

It was a fundamental assumption of Russell's, and one which he had taken over from the Millerites (a sect with which he had been briefly connected), that we are living in the last crucial days of this earth as we know it. He and his followers made it their basic conviction that the great conflict of Armageddon is in the *near* future and that following this, God will establish his thousand-year kingdom on this present earth. Once he had convinced himself of this, everything he found in the Bible or saw in the world around him, seemed to reinforce and support it. One seeming source of support was the series of remarkable discoveries, such as the 'Miracle

Wheat', the 'Millenial Bean', and the miraculous medical remedies already mentioned.

The 'Millenial Bean' is, in fact, a good example. It was discovered according to *Watchtower* (January 1912), by a Sister Smith of Nebraska. Wonderful powers were soon claimed for it and Sister Smith offered it to the Society as a means of raising funds. However, the Society (which had learned from some earlier episodes to be wary of public opinion) decided that it would not be wise to sell the seed, but announced that five bean seeds would be sent to any member of the Society who applied for them. Readers were advised to make hills six feet apart and to plant one seed to the hill; they were then to look for a truly wonderful harvest. Five beans, it was said, would provide sufficient for the needs of a small family.

The 'Millennial Bean' was just one of many 'signs' acclaimed by Pastor Russell. It must be admitted that when Mr Rutherford took over the leadership he repudiated some of his predecessor's teaching. The nonsense about the Great Pyramid, for example. He was trenchant enough about Russell to offend some of the latter's adherents, and a considerable number broke away from the organisation.

But Mr Rutherford had his own eccentricities. He looked at the world of his day and he exclaimed that he could see all around him the signs of the coming Millenium. He was incautious enough to list them in one of his books and they read as follows:

> Adding machines, aeroplanes, aluminium, antiseptic surgery, automatic couplers, automobiles, barbed wire, bicycles, carborundum, cash registers, celluloid, correspondence schools, cream separators, Darkest Africa, disk plows, Divine plan of the ages, dynamite, electric railways, electric welding, escalators, fireless cookers, gas engines, harvesting machines, illuminating gas, induction motors, linotypes, match machines, monotypes, motion pictures, North Pole, Panama Canal, pasteurization, radium, railway signals, Röntgen rays, shoe-sewing machines, skyscrapers, smokeless powder, South Pole, submarines, subways, talking machines, telephones, television, typewriters, vacuum cleaners, wireless telegraphy.

The Organisation also teaches that, as a prelude to the End, we can expect war and rumours of wars, famines and earthquakes, and all manner of natural disasters.

For the Witnesses, then, everything in the world and in the Bible—and especially in the Bible—is to be seen as evidence of on the one hand Armageddon and, on the other, a thousand years of bliss for the chosen ones.

All that they proclaim, their message and their methods, are determined by the conviction that there is not much longer to wait. Mankind, say the JWs, is on the brink.

They Misinterpret Scripture

Is it possible that the JWs are right? Can it be that after 2,000 years they really *are* the only ones accredited by God to interpret the Bible, and to declare to mankind what it really means?

The JWs are not the only sect to maintain on the one hand, that the Bible is inspired and infallible, and on the other hand, to claim to interpret the poetic imagery of such books as Ezekiel, Daniel and Revelation in a private and arbitrary way. These books have intrigued and fascinated many would-be interpreters, and many have succumbed to the temptation of identifying the characters, images and monsters with figures from current history. In different centuries men have found Napoleon, Hitler and others, where St John the Divine was depicting political monsters of his own day.

One of the groups which has claimed to interpret the enigmatic imagery of the Bible is that known as British Israel. They will give us a useful parallel to the beliefs of the Witnesses, even though they share very different assumptions and conclusions. Their general belief is (or was) that when the Israelite nation was led captive into Assyria, between 743–722 B.C., ten of the tribes got 'lost' and that the greater part of these ten tribes made their way across Europe under the names of Scythians and Kimmerians, etc. Finally, as Angles, Saxons, Celts, Danes and Normans, they arrived in the British Isles to become the British nation which, with the American peoples, is destined by God to rule the world in preparation for the Millenium. The tribe of Dan (so it is said) reached Ireland and became the Irish, and Manasseh (styled the 'Bowman' of Israel) became the ancestor of the American peoples. The American Eagle unconsciously witnesses to this: it holds a bunch of arrows in its left claw.

The British Israelites find in the Bible evidence of their strange belief. This is in spite of the fact that it is supported by no reputable independent biblical scholar nor, it should be said, by any historian or philologist.

They depend a great deal on pseudo-history and pseudo-philology, as we shall shortly see. It is said, for example, that one of the Hebrew words for a bull is ENGL, and this is clearly seen in the word England; the fact that our national symbol is John Bull is too great to be mere coincidence.

It is also pointed out that the Hebrew for 'covenant' is BRIT(H) and for man is ISH and one has only to put these two syllables together to construct the word 'British'.

They will take a chapter of the Bible and explain that it has a hidden meaning, provided that you use the code which they provide. In Ezekiel 38, for example, it is necessary to note that Gog is Russia, Meshek is Moscow, Tubal is Tobalsk, Gomer is Germany and Togarmah is Turkey. Having done this, one can show that the chapter refers to the twentieth century rather than to the century of Ezekiel, and confidently predict its future course.

When, in Jeremiah 33: 17, we read 'David shall never lack a man to sit on the throne of the House of Israel', the British Israelite assumed that this refers to King George VI whom (they claim by an intricate and unsubstantiated genealogical table) was a descendant of David.

The British Israelites did not neglect the Great Pyramid in their search for corroboration of their theories, and one of them, writing at the turn of the century, appealed to its measurements as well as to the Bible in order to produce the following prophecies with definite dates: 1919, Russia invades Palestine: 1920, War proclaimed in Europe: 1922, Universal famine: 1924, Jews return to Palestine: 1932, St Peter's Rome destroyed by fire; Pope and bishops perish.

This has been quoted at length because it is typical of this kind of interpretation, that the Bible should be treated as a code to be 'cracked'. It is not far removed from John Allegro's thesis that the Old and New Testaments form a complicated and disguised tract, advocating hallucinogenic mushrooms.

To treat the Bible in this way is irrational and illogical, but it holds a peculiar fascination for a certain type of mind. And JWs have got carried away with it. They will assert that 'the abomination of desolation'

(Matthew 24: 14) refers to the United Nations, that the beast in Revelation 13: 1 is the Roman Catholic Church, and (the British Israelites would not like this) that another beast is the British Empire.

When talking to JWs, as to other sectarians who use the Bible in an arbitrary way, it is as well to avoid the bandying about of scriptural texts. One text can always be found to match another and it can make discussion both interminable and confused, but perhaps one can be forgiven for quoting this one: 'No prophesy of scripture is a matter of one's own interpretation.' (1 Peter 1: 20, RSV.)

It should be realised that the Bible is a book which has been brought into being (under God) by the church, and it comes to us with the church's authorisation. It is a matter of history that the church, by a mixture of formal and informal means, decided what books were to be included in scripture and what were to be excluded from it. If any part of the Bible calls for particular interpretation, it is for the church to be the interpreter.

It is curious that the New World Society accepts the canon of scripture as set out by the Protestant part of the church, apparently without question. It would seem unreasonable to accept the Bible while ignoring or rejecting the authority from which it comes.

The Bible is a big enough book for people to find within its texts and phrases that which can be held to justify this or that eccentric teaching; it contains enough powerful imagery and poetry to stimulate fruitful and sometimes monstrous growths. The JWs are not the first to misuse scripture, and they will not, one imagines, be the last.

3

WHAT WE HAVE TO LEARN

SO far, our glance at the teachings of the New World Society will have shown us that it adopts a fantastic, bizarre and monstrous parody of what the Bible teaches. Yet we can hardly fail to be impressed by the rapid growth of this remarkable Movement, how in the hundred years of its existence it has achieved a total of over a million and a half active members in nearly every country of the world. It must surprise us that it can call out unsuspected talents from its members and evoke a degree of dedication that few denominations can claim to equal.

The natural response from the ordinary instructed Christian must be 'Their message is false—it must be their method and presentation which have achieved such a result.' This is partly, but not entirely true. There is something in their religion, false and irrational though it may be, which uncovers gifts in quite ordinary people. Perhaps the churches have made the Christian religion too smooth and too respectable; it was not so at the beginning when the smooth, the respectable and the privileged were affronted, first by Jesus, and later by the apostles of the early church. Perhaps there needs to be, on the threshold of religious commitment, a stumbling-block which causes a man to pause and say, 'This is impossible and incredible!' before he can truly go on to say, 'I believe'.

There is certainly an opinion, held by some Christians of commendable modesty, which attributes the success of any heresy or off-beat sect, to some defect in the church's teaching. It is said that when the church has failed to preach the total gospel and neglected some aspect of the faith, an unauthorised group has usually arisen, seized on the neglected factor and exalted it as if it were the heart and centre of the faith. If the church had faithfully witnessed to the gospel's stress on healing, there would have been no Christian Science; if the church had faithfully taught about the after-life and the communion of saints, spiritualism would never have arisen.

By this token the church 'deserves' the sects and heresies which rise up to plague and sometimes rival it. And they provide for the church a warning signal as to the gaps in her gospel. JWs point to five neglected aspects of the church's teaching:

1 It has failed to proclaim, in terms that modern man can understand, God's redemption of creation.
2 It has concentrated on individual and personal salvation and neglected the saved and saving community.
3 It has relied far too much on its clergy and has not emphasised that every Christian is and must be an active minister.
4 It has not trained its laity for service to any great extent.
5 It has not given to modern man a vision which helps him to understand the Bible as God's word to man in the world of today.

Through the Witnesses, it may be that God is calling his church to think again and to fill the gaps, to preach the total gospel of our Lord and Saviour Jesus Christ.

Further to this there are another five aspects of the life of the JWs which ought to make Christians re-examine their own life and the life of their churches.

1 *They have a sense of urgency* Dr Johnson said: 'Depend upon it, Sir, when a man knows he is to be hanged in a fortnight, it concentrates his mind wonderfully.' Their conviction that Armageddon is almost upon us and that this present world is near its end gives JWs a sense of urgency which must be similar to that which invigorated the Christians of New Testament times. 'There is no time to be wasted', say the JWs, and so they take every opportunity to go out and win converts.

2 *They have a good organisation* The organisation of the churches has developed in a haphazard way over the years, in some cases over the centuries, and badly needs an overhaul. The New World Society is more like a purpose-built structure which exists to proclaim what they believe about God's Kingdom. In particular, each congregation is small enough and compact enough to be effective among the members and a 'back-sliding' brother can be quickly noticed and encouraged back. Congregations are

small enough to make it possible for members really to care for each other. At the same time, the regular assemblies, at circuit, district and national level, enable the individual publisher to be (as they say) 'part of Jehovah's wonderful New World Society'. This Society is like a great family, a household with Jehovah as Head.

3 *They exercise stewardship* In the churches of this generation there is a great deal of talk about stewardship—resources must be used to the fullest possible extent, how important it is to exercise stewardship of money, time, skill and manpower. In the Society they do not talk about Stewardship, they actually practise it. Their members are active in preaching and publishing but other skills are put to good use. It is not unusual for their place of worship to have been built by the members, and it is their normal practice to share in the work of caretaking, maintenance and repairs of their property. JWs do not make the mistake, common in the churches, of demanding too little of their members. There is the further point that, although they have their Kingdom Halls, they make a practice of using the homes of members and 'prospects' whenever possible. This makes good use of resources, but it also makes a firm bridge between their religion and secular life, and it keeps them integrated. Sometimes the churches are aware of an unfortunate tendency to distinguish between the sacred and the secular and they have to remind themselves that life is a whole and God is supreme over all. It might be that further exploration into stewardship would make this reminder unnecessary.

4 *They never stop teaching* Every meeting, whether formal or informal, is a meeting for intensive instruction. Members are expected to prepare for their Sunday meetings by reading through the *Watchtower* article, checking Bible references and working out answers to the questions of which they have advance knowledge. At the meetings themselves, there is good congregational participation. They are supported by the knowledge that the same teaching is being promulgated everywhere in the world at the same time. Their teaching on the content of belief is backed up by an effective weekly instruction on 'how to put it across'. Instruction in personal evangelism is given practical application in that JWs go from door to door in twos; one of the pair is usually a learner under instruction. A Kingdom Hall is not regarded as fully equipped unless it has a library: this is an example that the churches would be wise to follow.

5 *They accept children and the home* We have seen that they like to operate within the home, and they carry out Bible studies there. The Society gives wise advice to its publishers: 'When children are sitting in, include them in your remarks; say some things they will understand. Let them read scripture references if they are old enough. Paraphrase your questions so they will get the sense of them, and occasionally ask them questions to which the answer is obvious, so they can get a start in answering.' Children are expected to attend the public meetings with their parents and although the speaker is sensitive to their presence (following the advice above) he rarely if ever 'talks down' to them. Parents customarily instruct their own children in their faith and regard it as remarkable that in the denominations this duty is passed on to Sunday School teachers. 'How can you hand over this solemn responsibility to some other person whom you hardly know?' they ask. Not all Christians will approve their practice of encouraging children to be active publishers at the earliest opportunity, but there is no doubt that the children appreciate the trust that is put in them.

4

POINTS TO REMEMBER

WHEN you are considering what to say to a JW there are fourteen points to bear in mind:

Introduction

1 First of all understand that he wants to convert you and that this is his sole object in calling. His immediate aim is to get you to take some of his literature, and later make a 'back-call' to get you to do Bible study on a pattern programmed by the Society.

2 It follows that he will try to set the pace, take the initiative and provide the agenda. He is trained to point out various texts which provide admirable platforms for JW doctrine which then emerges as if it had flowed straight from the Bible.

3 A number of these texts are quite obscure to us today and even our best biblical scholars do not know what they mean. Many of them refer to happenings in the writer's own day, thousands of years back, and have no relevance to the twentieth century or to the future. It is nonsense to pretend that they have.

4 Having said this, you will realise that it is disastrous to argue about particular texts. The JW is well-briefed and he probably knows his Bible better than you do.

The Authority of the Bible

5 Ask him why his Society assumes that the Bible is the word of God. Who told Russell or Rutherford that it was? Who put the Bible together

as a collection of sixty-six books? Press him hard on this. It is one basic question to which he has no answer.

6 The Bible is, in fact, the church's book. It was written by members of the church (Old and New) and it was the church which decided what books should be included in the Bible and which should be excluded.

7 When you have got this far you are nearly home. For the authority of the Bible is based on the authority of the church and if you reject the latter how can you accept the former?

8 To continue, the Bible is not self-evident as God's book unless you accept the witness of the church. The trustworthiness of your local newspaper is not separate and distinct from the editor and staff which produce it.

Keep Conversation General

9 Consequently it is suggested that you give a warm welcome to the JW visitor when he comes to see you. You might offer him a cup of tea or coffee; a glass of beer could work wonders. Then talk about the weather or the state of the harvest. Talk about everything but religion. Ask him about his family—he may be a JW, but he is a human being as well.

10 The danger is that you will be drawn into discussing particular texts. This will (if you are doing well) tempt you to 'score points' as if your visitor were an opponent or (if you are doing badly) cause you to despair and capitulate.

Introduce him to the Church

11 You should have an aim, too. So your next step is to ask him to come to your church for a service. The chances of his agreeing to this are slender in the extreme, but it is vital that you should keep the initiative.

12 When you go to church, assuming that he has agreed, arrange to meet him at the door or, better still, to call for him. Arrange with some of your friends in the congregation to be on the look-out for you both and to greet him warmly and give him a welcome. Make sure, too, that your church is the cheerful, friendly, loving community in which a stranger will feel at home.

Tell him what you Believe

13 Ask him to have a meal with you and set aside time to talk to him about what you believe. Do you feel that this is a laborious and time-consuming process and one which you would be unwilling to undertake with a JW caller? Then reflect! He would not hesitate to take similar trouble over you.

14 If you decide that getting involved with a JW is too much trouble it is probably better to turn him away when he first comes to the door with his companion. But if you do, it is a sign that he reflects more credit on his Organisation than you do on your church.